Penguin Modern Poets
VOLUME 8

Jackie Kay was born in Edinburgh in 1961 and brought up in Scotland. She received an Honours Degree in English from the University of Stirling in 1983. Her first collection of poetry, *The Adoption Papers* (Bloodaxe, 1991), was originally broadcast on Radio 3 as part of the *Drama Now* series. She has written several plays, including most recently *Twilight Shift* (1994), which won an Edinburgh Evening News Festival Award. She writes poetry for children, and *Two's Company* and *Three Has Gone* are both published by Puffin. Her second collection of poetry for adults, *Other Lovers* (Bloodaxe, 1993), received the Somerset Maugham award.

Merle Collins is from Grenada and came to Britain in 1983. Until 1995 she taught Caribbean Studies at the University of North London. She now lives in the United States and teaches Caribbean Literature and Creative Writing at the University of Maryland. Her publications include two novels, *Angel* and *The Colour of Forgetting*, two poetry collections, *Because the Dawn Breaks* and *Rotten Pomerack*, and a collection of short stories, *Rain Darling*.

Grace Nichols was born and brought up in Guyana. She came to Britain in 1977 and lives in Lewes with her family. She won the 1983 Commonwealth Poetry Prize for her collection *I is a Long-memoried Woman*, which was followed by *The Fat Black Woman's Poems* and *Lazy Thoughts of a Lazy Woman*. Grace Nichols has also written poetry for children, including *Come On into My Tropical Garden* and *Give Yourself a Hug*. Her first novel, *Whole of a Morning Sky*, was published in 1986 and looks at pre-independence Guyana, the landscape of her childhood. She has edited popular anthologies, including *Poetry Jump Up, Can I Buy a Slice of Sky?* and *A Caribbean Dozen*. Her most recent collection is *SUNRIS*, published by Virago.

The Penguin Modern Poets Series

Penguin Modern Poets

VOLUME 8

JACKIE KAY

· MERLE COLLINS

GRACE NICHOLS

PENGUIN BOOKS

Published by the Penguin Group
Penguin Books Ltd, 27 Wrights Lane, London w8 5tz, England
Penguin Books USA Inc., 375 Hudson Street, New York, New York 10014, USA
Penguin Books Australia Ltd, Ringwood, Victoria, Australia
Penguin Books Canada Ltd, 10 Alcorn Avenue, Toronto, Ontario, Canada m4v 3b2
Penguin Books (NZ) Ltd, 182–190 Wairau Road, Auckland 10, New Zealand

Penguin Books Ltd, Registered Office: Harmondsworth, Middlesex, England

This selection first published 1996
10 9 8 7 6 5 4 3 2 1

Set in 10.5/14 pt Monotype Garamond
Typeset by Datix International Limited, Bungay, Suffolk
Printed in England by Clays Ltd, St Ives plc

Contents

Jackie Kay

My Grandmother

My grandmother is like a Scottish pine
Tall straight-backed, proud and plentiful
A fine head of hair, greying now
Tied up in a loose bun
Her face is ploughed land
Her eyes shine rough as amethysts
She wears a plaid shawl
Of our clan with the zeal of an Amazon
She is one of those women –
Burnt in her croft, rather than moved off the land
She comes from them, her snake's skin
She speaks Gaelic mostly, English only
When she has to, then it's blasphemy

My grandmother sits by the fire and swears
There'll be no Darkie baby in this house

My grandmother is a Scottish pine
Tall straight-backed, proud and plentiful
Her hair tied with pins in a ball of steel wool
Her face is tight as ice
And her eyes are amethysts.

from THE ADOPTION PAPERS

THE WAITING LISTS

The first agency we went to
didn't want us on their lists
we didn't live close enough to a church
nor were we church-goers
(though we kept quiet about being communists).
The second told us
we weren't high enough earners.
The third liked us
but they had a five-year waiting list.
I spent six months trying not to look
at swings nor the front of the supermarket trolleys,
not to think this kid I've wanted could be five.
The fourth agency was full up.
The fifth said yes but again no babies.
Just as we were going out the door
I said oh you know we don't mind the colour.
Just like that, the waiting was over.

This morning a slim manila envelope arrives
postmarked Edinburgh: one piece of paper.
I have now been able to look up your microfiche
(as this is all the records kept nowadays).
From your mother's letters, the following information:
Your mother was nineteen when she had you.
You weighed eight pounds four ounces.
She liked hockey. She worked in Aberdeen
as a waitress. She was five foot eight inches.

I thought I'd hid everything
that there wasnie wan
giveaway sign left

I put Marx Engels Lenin (no Trotsky)
in the airing cupboard – she'll no be
checking out the towels surely

All the copies of the *Daily Worker*
I shoved under the sofa
the dove of peace I took down from the loo

A poster of Paul Robeson
saying give him his passport
I took down from the kitchen

I left a bust of Burns
my detective stories
and the *Complete Works of Shelley*

She comes at 11.30 exactly.
I pour her coffee
from my new Hungarian set

And foolishly pray she willnae
ask its origins – honestly
this baby is going to my head.

She crosses her legs on the sofa
I fancy I hear the *Daily Workers*
rustle underneath her

Well she says, you have an interesting home
She sees my eyebrows rise.
It's different she qualifies.

Hell and I've spent all morning
trying to look ordinary
– a lovely home for the baby.

She buttons her coat all smiles
I'm thinking
I'm on the home run

But just as we get to the last post
her eye catches at the same times as mine
a red ribbon with twenty world peace badges

Clear as a hammer and sickle
on the wall.
Oh, she says are you against nuclear weapons?

To Hell with this. Baby or no baby.
Yes I says. Yes yes yes.
I'd like this baby to live in a nuclear free world.

Oh. Her eyes light up.
I'm all for peace myself she says,
and sits down for another cup of coffee.

BABY LAZARUS

Land moves like driven cattle
My eyes snatch pieces of news
headlines strung out on a line:
MOTHER DROWNS BABY IN THE CLYDE

November

The social worker phoned,
our baby is a girl but not healthy
she won't pass the doctor's test
until she's well. The adoption papers
can't be signed. I put the phone down.
I felt all hot. Don't get overwrought.
What does she expect? I'm not a mother
until I've signed that piece of paper.

The rhythm of the train carries me
over the frigid earth
the constant chug a comforter
a rocking cradle.

Maybe the words lie
across my forehead
headline in thin ink:
MOTHER GIVES BABY AWAY

December

We drove to Edinburgh,
I was that excited the forty miles
seemed a lifetime. What do you think she'll
look like? I don't know my man says. I could tell
he was as nervous as me. On the way back his face
was one long smile even although
he didn't get inside. Only me.
I wore a mask but she didn't seem to mind
I told her *any day now my darling any day.*

Nobody would ever guess.
I had no other choice
Anyway it's best for her,
My name signed on a dotted line.

March

Our baby has passed.
We can pick her up in two days.
Two days for Christ's sake,
could they not have given us a bit more notice?

Land moves like driven cattle

I must stop it. Put it out my mind.
There is no use going over and over.
I'm glad she's got a home to go to.
This sandwich is plastic.

I forgot to put sugar in the flask.
The man across the table keeps staring.
I should have brought another book —
all this character does is kiss and say sorry

go and come back
we are all foolish with trust.
I used to like winter
the empty spaces, the fresh air.

When I got home
I went out into the garden —
the frost bit my old brown boots —
and dug a hole the size of my baby
and buried the clothes I'd bought anyway.
A week later I stood at my window
and saw the ground move and swell
the promise of a crop,
that's when she started crying.
I gave her a service then, sang
Ye banks and braes, planted
a bush of roses, read the Book of Job,
cursed myself digging a pit for my baby
sprinkling ash from the grate.

Late that same night
she came in by the window,
my baby Lazarus
and suckled at my breast.

THE TWEED HAT DREAM

Today I ring the counselling agency in Edinburgh.
Can you start to trace through marriage certificates?
It will take three weeks what do you expect from it.
If she wants to meet me that's fine if she doesn't
that is also fine.

This morning the counselling woman rings
she's found someone who might be her
she's not sure; do I know my grandmother's name?
Pity. She'll be in touch, not sure when.

Her mother just turns up at the door
with a tweed hat on. I thinks
she doesn't suit tweed, she's too young.
In all these months I've never put a face to her
that looks like my daughter – so picture me
when I see those lips. She looks a dead spit
except of course she's white; lightning white.
She says in her soft Highland voice
can you let me see her? Can you?
What could I do? She comes in swift
as wind in a storm, rushes up the stairs
as if she knows the house already,
picks up my baby and strokes her cheeks endlessly
till I get tired and say, I'll be downstairs.

I put the kettle on, maybe
hot tea will redden those white cheeks,
arrange a plate of biscuits which keep
sliding onto the floor.
She's been up there helluva long.
I don't know where the thought comes from
but suddenly I'm pounding the stairs
like thunder. Her tweed hat
is in the cot. That is all.

That night I turn it through till dawn
a few genes, blood, a birth.
All this bother, certificates, papers.
It is all so long ago. Does it matter?
Now I come from her,
the mother who stole my milk teeth
ate the digestive left for Santa.

BLACK BOTTOM

Maybe that's why I don't like
all this talk about her being black,
I brought her up as my own
as I would any other child
colour matters to the nutters;
but she says my daughter says
it matters to her.

I suppose there would have been things
I couldn't understand with any child,
we knew she was coloured.
They told us they had no babies at first
and I chanced it didn't matter what colour it was
and they said *oh well are you sure*

in that case we have a baby for you –
to think she wasn't even thought of as a baby,
my baby, my baby

I chase his *Sambo Sambo* all the way from the school gate.
A fistful of anorak – What did you call me? Say that again.
Sam-bo. He plays the word like a bouncing ball
but his eyes move fast as ping pong.
I shove him up against the wall,
say that again you wee shite. *Sambo, sambo,* he's crying now

I knee him in the balls. What was that?
My fist is steel; I punch and punch his gut.
Sorry I didn't hear you? His tears drip like wax.
Nothing he heaves *I didn't say nothing.*
I let him go. He is a rat running. He turns
and shouts *Dirty Darkie.* I chase him again.
Blond hairs in my hand. Excuse me!
This teacher from primary 7 stops us.
Names? I'll report you to the headmaster tomorrow.
But Miss. Save it for Mr Thompson she says

My teacher's face cracks into a thin smile
Her long nails scratch the note well well
I see you were fighting yesterday, again.
In a few years' time you'll be a juvenile delinquent.
Do you know what that is? Look it up in the dictionary.
She spells each letter with slow pleasure.
Read it out to the class.
Thug. Vandal. Hooligan. Speak up! Have you lost your tongue?

To be honest I hardly ever think about it
except if something happens, you know
daft talk about darkies. Racialism.
Mothers ringing my bell with their kids
crying *You tell. You tell. You tell.*
– *No*. You tell your little girl to stop calling
my little girl names and I'll tell my little girl
to stop giving your little girl a doing.

We're practising for the school show
I'm trying to do the Cha Cha and the Black Bottom
but I can't get the steps right
my right foot's left and my left foot's right
my teacher shouts from the bottom
of the class Come on, show

us what you can do, I thought
you people had it in your blood.
My skin is hot as burning coal
like that time she said Darkies are like coal
in front of the whole class – my blood
what does she mean? I thought

she'd stopped all that after the last time
my dad talked to her on parents' night
the other kids are all right till she starts;
my feet step out of time, my heart starts
to miss beats like when I can't sleep at night –
What is in My Blood? The bell rings, it is time.

THE PHONE CALL

I have had my grandmother's Highland number
for four months now burning a hole in my filofax.

Something this morning gives me courage
to close the kitchen door and dial.

My grandmother's voice sounds much younger
'I used to work ages ago with your daughter

Elizabeth, do you have her present address?'
Sorry, she says, *No, but one of the girls*

will have it. She gives me another Highland number
wishing me luck. *What did you say your name was?*

Thirty minutes later my mother's sister
asks lots of questions – *Where did you work?*

How long ago was that? What age are you?
Forty I lie. *For a minute I thought . . .*

But if you're forty, you can't be.
I know she knows. The game's a bogey.

Actually I'm 26. *I thought so, love.*
I thought it was you. Mam knew too.

She just rang to warn me you'd ring.
How are you? How's your life been?

I'll give her yours. She'll write.
I'm sure you understand. I do. I do.

Now she's gone. I get phone calls regularly.
It's not that I think I'm losing out but
I've surprised myself just the same;

I've had to stop myself saying, 'Drop
it, you'll get hurt.' I do worry
of course I do, but it's me that's hurt.
Tonight I cried watching bloody Adam
Carrington discover he's not a Carrington
any more. Daft. Getting myself into a tizzy.

THE MEETING DREAM

If I picture it like this it hurts less
We are both shy
though our eyes are not,
they pierce below skin.
We are not as we imagined:
I am smaller, fatter, darker
I am taller, thinner
and I'd always imagined her hair dark brown
not grey. I can see my chin in hers
that is all, though no doubt
my mum will say, when she looks at the photo,
she's your double she really is.

There is no sentiment in this living-room,
a plain wood table and a few books.
We don't cuddle or even shake hands
though we smile sudden as a fire blazing
then die down.
Her hands play with her wedding-ring,
I've started smoking again.

We don't ask big questions even later by the shore.
We walk slow, tentative as crabs
No, so what have you been doing the past 26 years.
Just what are you working at, stuff like that

Ages later I pick up a speckled stone
and hurl it into the sea,
is this how you imagined it to be?
I never imagined it.

Oh. I hear the muffled splash.
It would have driven me mad imagining,
26 years is a long time.

Inside once more I sip hot tea
notice one wood-framed photo.
The air is as old as the sea.
I stare at her chin till she makes me look down.
Her hands are awkward as rocks.
My eyes are stones washed over and over.

If I picture it like this it hurts less

One dream cuts another open like a gutted fish
nothing is what it was;
she is too many imaginings to be flesh and blood.
There is nothing left to say.
Neither of us mentions meeting again.

Brendon Gallacher

For my brother, Maxie

He was seven and I was six, my Brendon Gallacher.
He was Irish and I was Scottish, my Brendon Gallacher.
His father was in prison; he was a cat burglar.
My father was a communist party full-time worker.
He has six brothers and I had one, my Brendon Gallacher.

He would hold my hand and take me by the river
Where we'd talk all about his family being poor.
He'd get his mum out of Glasgow when he got older.
A wee holiday someplace nice. Someplace far.
I'd tell my mum about my Brendon Gallacher

How his mum drank and his daddy was a cat burglar.
And she'd say, 'Why not have him round to dinner?'
No, no, I'd say, he's got big holes in his trousers.
I like meeting him by the burn in the open air.
Then one day after we'd been friends two years,

One day when it was pouring and I was indoors,
My mum says to me, 'I was talking to Mrs Moir
Who lives next door to your Brendon Gallacher
Didn't you say his address was 24 Novar?
She says there are no Gallachers at 24 Novar

There never have been any Gallachers next door.'
And he died then, my Brendon Gallacher,
Flat out on my bedroom floor, his spiky hair,
His impish grin, his funny flapping ear.
Oh Brendon. Oh my Brendon Gallacher.

Sassenachs

Me and my best pal (well, she was
till a minute ago) are off to London.
First trip on an InterCity alone.
When we got on we were the same
kind of excited – jigging on our seats,
staring at everyone. But then,
I remembered I was to be sophisticated.
So when Jenny starts shouting,
'Look at that, the land's flat already,'
when we are just outside Glasgow
(Motherwell actually) I feel myself flush.
Or even worse, 'Sassenach country.
Wey Hey Hey.' The tartan tammy
sitting proudly on top of her pony;
the tartan scarf swinging like a tail.
The nose pressed to the window.
'England's not so beautiful, is it?'
And we haven't even crossed the border.
And the train's jazzy beat joins her:
Sassenachs sassenachs here we come.
Sassenachs sassenachs Rum Tum Tum.
Sassenachs sassenachs how do you do.
Sassenachs sassenachs we'll get you.
Then she loses momentum, so out come
the egg mayonnaise sandwiches and
the big bottle of bru. 'Ma ma's done us proud,'
says Jenny, digging in, munching loud.
The whole train is an egg and I'm inside it.
I try and remain calm; Jenny starts it again,
Sassenachs sassenachs Rum Tum Tum.

Finally, we get there: London, Euston;
and the very first person on the platform
gets asked – 'Are you a genuine sassenach?'
I want to die, but instead I say, Jenny.
He replies in that English way –
'I beg your pardon,' and Jenny screams
'Did you hear that Voice?'
And we both die laughing, clutching
our stomachs at Euston station.

In My Country

walking by the waters
down where an honest river
shakes hands with the sea,
a woman passed round me
in a slow watchful circle,
as if I were a superstition;

or the worst dregs of her imagination,
so when she finally spoke
her words spliced into bars
of an old wheel. A segment of air.
'Where do you come from?'
'Here,' I said. 'Here. These parts.'

The Red Graveyard

There are some stones that open in the night like flowers
Down in the red graveyard where Bessie haunts her lovers.
There are stones that shake and weep in the heart of the night
Down in the red graveyard where Bessie haunts her lovers.

Why do I remember the blues?
I am five or six or seven in the back garden;
the window is wide open;
her voice is slow motion through the heavy summer air.
Jelly roll. Kitchen man. Sausage roll. Frying pan.

Inside the house where I used to be myself,
her voice claims the rooms. In the best room even,
something has changed the shape of my silence.
Why do I remember her voice and not my own mother's?
Why do I remember the blues?

My mother's voice. What was it like?
A flat stone for skitting. An old rock.
Long long grass. Asphalt. Wind. Hail.
Cotton. Linen. Salt. Treacle.
I think it was a peach.
I heard it down to the ribbed stone.

I am coming down the stairs in my father's house.
I am five or six or seven. There is fat thick wallpaper
I always caress, bumping flower into flower.
She is singing. (Did they play anyone else ever?)
My father's feet tap a shiny beat on the floor.

Christ, my father says, that's some voice she's got.
I pick up the record cover. And now. This is slow motion.
My hand swoops, glides, swoops again.
I pick up the cover and my fingers are all over her face.
Her black face. Her magnificent black face.
That's some voice. His shoes dancing on the floor.

There are some stones that open in the night like flowers
Down in the red graveyard where Bessie haunts her lovers.
There are stones that shake and weep in the heart of night
Down in the red graveyard where Bessie haunts her lovers.

Blues

Hell, I can't even take my own advice,
that's what she thought often, when her left eye
(always the left) was swollen and a blue river
ran underneath the brown; or when
whole parts of her body could not
be walked on, or swam in, or touched even.
When her body had no-go areas; something-only areas.
Danger: a fence right round her skin, wooden
as her own voice the morning after

all that violence. It was in the way they looked at her.
It was not in her mind. She did not grow such looks
in her own backyard. The hard stare; the furtive one where
the eyes were a fast car swerving as she walked near.
Nothing could persuade her not to be funny.
She could not stop being funny. Making people
laugh till they cried, hurt themselves, howl.
She was a shouter. She could barrelhouse.
But on the morning after all that violence

she could not raise the roof of her voice.
She could not embellish or endow or growl.
Laugh, yes. Grunt. Giggle. Once she caught herself
in the trembling mirror. *A minstrel.*
She tried to be completely still.
As if she were committing a murder.
A clown. An aunt jemima. She had a smile
that could cross a river. And she had a laugh
that could build a raft. And that was all she had.

Twelve Bar Bessie

See that day, Lord, did you hear what happened then.
A nine o'clock shadow always chases the sun.
And in the thick heavy air came the Ku Klux Klan
To the tent where the Queen was about to sing her song.

They were going to pull the Blues Tent down.
Going to move the Queen out of the town.
Take her twelve bar beat and squash it into the ground.
She tried to get her Prop Boys together, and they got scared.

She tried to get the Prop Boys together, and they got scared.
She said Boys, Boys, get those men out of here.
But they ran away and left the Empress on her own.
She went up to the men who had masks over their head

With the hand on her hips she cursed and she hollered,
'I'll get the whole damn lot of you out of here now
If I have to. You're as good as dead.
You just pick up the sheets and run. Go on.'

That's what she done. Her voice was cast-iron.
You should have seen them. You should have seen them.
Those masks made of sheets from somebody's bed.
Those masks flying over their heads. Flapping.

They was flapping like some strange bird migrating.
Some bird that smelt danger in the air, a blue song.
And flew. Fast. Out of the small mid western town.
To the sound of black hands clapping.

And the Empress saying, 'And as for you' to the ones who did
    nothing.

Even the Trees

Even the trees outside feel it, their fine branches
their sixth sense of mercy,

they bend into the wind and ask for forgiveness
to come in a storm,

and join the congregation of silence; that tall witness.
One man, tied to a tree and whipped

never worked again in the cotton fields. In the early
light, the delicate bone-light

that broke hearts, a song swept from field to field;
a woman's memory paced centuries,

down and down, a blue song in the beat of her heart,
in an old car that crossed

a railroad track; the scream of a warning –
is that why we remember certain things and not others;

the sound of the bass, the sound of the whip, the strange
strangled wind, bruises floating through light air

like leaves and landing, landing, here; this place.
Everything that's happened once could happen again.

Pounding Rain

News of us spreads like a storm.
The top of our town to the bottom.
We stand behind curtains
parted like hoods; watch each other's eyes.

We talk of moving to the west end,
this bit has always been a shoe box
tied with string; but then again
your father still lives in that house
where we warmed up spaghetti bolognese
in lunch hours and danced to Louis Armstrong,
his gramophone loud as our two heart beats
going boom diddy boom diddy boom.

Did you know then? I started dating Davy;
when I bumped into you I'd just say Hi.
I tucked his photo booth smile into my satchel
brought him out for my pals in the intervals.

A while later I heard you married Trevor Campbell.
Each night I walked into the school dinner hall
stark naked, till I woke to Miss, Miss Miss
every minute. Then, I bumped into you at the Cross.

You haven't changed you said; that reassurance.
Nor you; your laugh still crosses the street.
I trace you back, beaming, till –
Why don't you come round, Trevor would love it.

He wasn't in. I don't know how it happened.
We didn't bother with a string of do you remembers.
I ran my fingers through the beads in your hair.
Your hair's nice I said stupidly, nice, suits you.

We sat and stared till our eyes filled
like a glass of wine. I did it, the thing
I'd dreamt a million times. I undressed you
slowly, each item of clothing fell
with a sigh. I stroked your silk skin
until we were back in the Campsies, running
down the hills in the pounding rain,
screaming and laughing; soaked right through.

Dusting the Phone

I am spending my time imagining the worst that could happen.
I know this is not a good idea, and that being in love, I could
    be
spending my time going over the best that has been happening.

The phone rings heralding some disaster. Sirens.
Or it doesn't ring which also means disaster. Sirens.
In which case, who would ring me to tell? Nobody knows.

The future is a long gloved hand. An empty cup.
A marriage. A full house. One night per week
in stranger's white sheets. Forget tomorrow,

You say, don't mention love. I try. It doesn't work.
I assault the postman for a letter. I look for flowers.
I go over and over our times together, re-read them.

This very second I am waiting on the phone.
Silver service. I polish it. I dress for it.
I'll give it extra in return for your call.

Infuriatingly, it sends me hoaxes, wrong numbers;
or worse, calls from boring people. Your voice
disappears into my lonely cotton sheets.

I am trapped in it. I can't move. I want you.
All the time. This is awful – only a photo.
Come on, damn you, ring me. Or else. What?

I don't know what.

A Country Walk

In the dark afternoon light, we two walk
in the soft insistent rain, along the country road,
between two massive hedges no one can see over.

At the turn of the bend is the baby you long for:
a red head, a girl, her two small feet
running ahead of us. You are coming to her

a long way off. And the rain is harder,
soaking us right through. She calls
in the strange light; the sky a slate, wordless.

You fear her, me, our future. Suddenly
five magpies split in the sky like atoms.
The fields lose their boundaries.

The hedgerow gone. The smell of cowdung.
The black earth split open. She still waits.
Who is her father? Which country is her home?

All this is harder than the rain; us two together.
Than the dry stone dyke which guards the farm.
Or the grey sky that reveals no secret. No one

can tell us the way; we are miles off. At the turn
of the bend, a fairytale house stands, innocent.
Carved in stone. You could have that room;

I could have the east. We could both grow things.
Inside the small holiday house, we eat the bricks.
You light the fire. We sit in tender silence.

Only, your face is raw; thinking, thinking;
your eyes sweep the floor into the corner.
Your tongue is a silent poker stirring the fire.

Keeping Orchids

The orchids my mother gave me when we first met
are still alive, twelve days later. Although

some of the buds remain closed as secrets.
Twice since I carried them back, like a baby in a shawl,

from her train station to mine, then home. Twice
since then the whole glass carafe has crashed

falling over, unprovoked, soaking my chest of drawers.
All the broken waters. I have rearranged

the upset orchids with troubled hands. Even after
that the closed ones did not open out. The skin

shut like an eye in the dark; the closed lid.
Twelve days later, my mother's hands are all I have.

Her face is fading fast. Even her voice rushes
through a tunnel the other way from home.

I close my eyes and try to remember exactly:
a paisley pattern scarf, a brooch, a navy coat.

A digital watch her daughter was wearing when she died.
Now they hang their heads,

and suddenly grow old – the proof of the meeting. Still,
her hands, awkward and hard to hold

fold and unfold a green carrier bag as she tells
the story of her life. Compressed. Airtight.

A sad square, then a crumpled shape. A bag of tricks.
Her secret life – a hidden album, a box of love letters.

A door opens and closes. Time is outside waiting.
I catch the draught in my winter room.

Airlocks keep the cold air out.
Boiling water makes flowers live longer. So does

cutting the stems with a sharp knife.

Dance of the Cherry Blossom

Both of us are getting worse
Neither knows who had it first

He thinks I gave it to him
I think he gave it to me

Nights chasing clues where
One memory runs into another like dye.

Both of us are getting worse
I know I'm wasting precious time

But who did he meet between
May 87 and March 89.

I feel his breath on my back
A slow climb into himself, then out.

In the morning it all seems different
Neither knows who had it first

We eat breakfast together – newspapers
And silence except for the slow slurp of tea

This companionship is better than anything
He thinks I gave it to him.

By lunchtime we're fighting over some petty thing
He tells me I've lost my sense of humour

I tell him I'm not Glaswegian
You all think death is a joke

It's not funny. I'm dying for fuck's sake
I think he gave it to me.

Just think he says it's every couple's dream
I won't have to wait for you up there

I'll have you night after night – your glorious legs
Your strong hard belly, your kissable cheeks.

I cry when he says things like that
My shoulders cave in, my breathing trapped.

Do you think you have a corner on dying
You self-pitying wretch, pathetic queen.

He pushes me; we roll on the floor like whirlwind;
When we are done in, our lips find each other

We touch soft as breeze, caress the small parts
Rocking back and forth, his arms become mine.

There's nothing outside but the noise of the wind
The cherry blossom's dance through the night.

Dressing Up

For Toby

My family's all so squalid
I'm trying to put it behind
me – real typical working class
Scottish: Da beats Ma drinks it off.
I couldn't stomach it, banging

doors, turning ma music up top
blast. I told ma ma years ago. She'd
rather I murdered somebody than
that. She wasn't joking either.
Nobody gets hurt, it's not for

the image even I'm just dead
childish. Mascara I like, rouge,
putting it on after powder.
I love wearing lots of layers.
Ma ma always dresses boring.

No frills. See at Christmas I had
on black stockings Santa would kill
for and even Quentin Crisp would
look drab beside my beautiful
feather boa – bright fucking red.

Ma ma didn't touch her turkey.
Finally she said What did I do
I know what they call you, transvite.
You look a bloody mess you do.
She had a black eye, a navy dress.

Dracula

After we'd climbed the many roads from Efori Nord
by bus past Bucharest, the capital of Romania,
I was dog tired. We went to a mountain room of pine,

and I searched the cupboards before I fell asleep.
That night I heard this weird flapping
at the window and woke up scared to death.

There, on the verandah, was a figure in black.
Casting no shadow. My hand instinctively flew
to my neck. Count Dracula was born here.

The cotton sheets were soaking with my sweat.
I could see his eyes flashing as he bent down;
imagine the two small sinister holes in my skin.

If only we had stayed in Efori Nord,
playing ping pong till Kingdom come.
If only we hadn't come to the mountains.

I crawled along the pine floor to my father's bed.
It was empty. Just a white pillow and a headrest.
My dad gave a loud guffaw from the balcony.

Took off his black cape; threw back his head,
said, 'Got you going there, didn't I?
Okay. The joke's over. Back to your bed.'

Can you believe that? All I am asking is:
who needs an imagination, a fear, or a dread,
when what we've got is parents instead?

Going to See *King Lear*

On the big red smooth seat, I
watch the giant television
and my mother's eyes, greedy,
gulping everything down like
chocolate raisins. In front
of me are rows of heads that
put me in such a bad mood:

sleek shining page-boy, snobby
at the back; tight bossy bun,
trapped in a net; tall, selfish
beehive blocking my view. Then,
all of a sudden, darkness
comes down, sweet, and will not melt
in the hand or in the mouth.

I am sitting with strangers,
just the shapes and silhouettes
of them now. We breath in, all
of us, in one breath waiting
to be changed, to stop time or
for the trailer to end and
King Lear begin. No children,

except me, watching with mum,
who leans forward, her body,
diagonal, her fury
at good King Lear's disloyal
daughters, she whispers, 'Get out'
to the good one, Or 'Don't put
up with that.' (I think it was

Cordelia.) When King Lear's
Gloucester gets his eyes gouged out,
my mother falls off her chair.
I cover my eyes. Too late.
I've seen it. The terrible
tormenting sight of a man's
hands over his helpless, scooped

sockets, staggering back to
some other time of trust, whilst
those egg-whites of his eyes run.
'Vile jelly,' I shake, appalled.
Lear foams, whisked-white, at the mouth.
Jesus, my mother says, shocked,
That was good. That was so good.

Her eyes glint, green with pleasure.
Deep sigh when the names appear
and disappear. So slowly,
she rises from the red seat.
I had to see it. I did.
What a good, good girl, sitting
all quiet. My mouth has fallen

open for good. It won't close.
I am seven, I have seen
Lear's best friend get his eyes poked
out. The red floor is sliding
downwards. I will fall into
myself years later; grown-up,
velvet curtains drawn open.

I Try My Absolute Best

I give my kids pure apple juice
(no sugar less acid than orange)
buy my baby soya milk formula
now she's off the breast
(non-dairy, no cholesterol, good
for their little hearts – apparently
their arteries can harden before five
even). Water from the purifier.
Perrier if I'm feeling flush
(they can always pretend it's lemonade).
Carob-coated date bars. Cherry or banana.
And there's a shop down the street
that is selling organic vegetables
(no sprays, no chemicals).
Only to find the bloody English apples
are being sprayed with alar and are
carcinogenic; the soya beans are cooked
in aluminium pots which give off deposits
in the brain; the cartridge in the purifier
collects things (like knickers if they're not changed).
Perrier's got benzene in it, which gives rats
cancer. Though I personally don't know any rat
that drinks Perrier, do you? And them
so-called Health Food Bars contain more sugar
than the average Mars Bar. What's the use
in calling anything organic when
the bloody soil's chock-a-block with lead?

I try my absolute best
drink decaff coffee to pipe me down
instead of hype me up only to find
out from my eldest daughter
that what they put the beans through
is worse for you than an ordinary Nescafé.

I'm back on Valium.
My kids are stuffing Monster Munch
and Mars Bars down them.
My youngest son even ate a hamburger yesterday.
It's driving me crazy.
I says it's your pocket money,
do what you want with it.

Pork Pies

We're not together any more.
After Bobby Baxter followed us home,
drank our pop and ate our mini pork pies
(he had five) our whole life

changed. We kept him in our room
upstairs; taught him our special tongue,
watched him flash up on television.
Missing three days, four days, six, seven.

On the last day at ninety degrees Fahrenheit,
Robert James Baxter looked out our high window
and waved. He had been warned. Bad Bobby.
And some ugly nosy Parker looked

up, some pain-in-the-neck village golfer.
Putt Putt Putt. 999. A hole in one.
Next thing: the policeman at our door;
our mum there in her brassière,

the loose language of gin, opening
and closing her mouth; her eyes narrow
and fierce as a bird's; a seagull's fury,
calling us down, calling us down,

Hannah and Helen. Never Helen and Hannah,
we dressed in the same black patent leather
shoes, shining like mirrors. Our checked
gingham dress, its pink and green squares.

Our jet black hair parted in the same centre;
our east-coast identical accents, *well spoken*.
The village plodder held the picture in the air.
'Have you seen this boy?'

'No, sir,' we said together. Pause. 'No, sir.'
Big boys in blue searched our room,
but Bobby Baxter, beautiful Bobby Baxter,
wasn't found till five days later.

Got You

You know I am the shy one really, don't you,
not you; that your maths have my answers,
then how come I am the slow one

and you are the one who shines. School Dux.
Prefect. Your blazer is shabbier than mine
but Gran from Dornock loves you better

than me and so does our mother. The dog
licks you. People who say they can't tell
the difference drive you crazy: your skin is creamier,

your nose less wide; your hair loose floppy
curls, not *frizzy*, not *sheep's wool*. I know,
I know like I know the back of my hand. Last night

in the top bunk, I wanted to climb down
and do something. Can't tell what. Not even in our tongue.
I swallowed hard listening for the sound of real sleep

till I must have given in again.
You know me better than I know you.
Always get me. I sat bolt upright, my heart

flapped like our bedroom curtains, your night-time
laughter, soft, squeezed to your chest, doubled-up:
'Got you. Didn't I. Got you again.'

Attention Seeking

I'm needing attention.
I know I'm needing attention
because I hear people say it.
People that know these things.
I'm needing attention,
so what I'll do is steal something.
I know I'll steal something
because that is what I do
when I'm needing attention.
Or else I'll mess up my sister's room,
throw all her clothes onto the floor,
put her gerbil under her pillow
and lay a trap above the door
a big heavy dictionary to drop on her
when she comes through. (Swot.)
This is the kind of thing I do
when I'm needing attention.
But I'm never boring.
I always think up new things.
Attention has lots of colours
and tunes. And lots of punishments.
For attention you can get detention.
Extra homework. Extra housework.
All sorts of things. Although
yesterday I heard the woman say
that I was just needing
someone to listen. My dad went mad.
'Listen to him!' he said. 'Listen!
You've got to be joking.'

Mind you that was right after
I stole his car keys and drove
his car straight into the wall.
I wasn't hurt, but I'm still
needing quite a lot of attention.

The School Hamster's Holiday

Remember the coal bunker in winter?
Naw? You wouldn't want to, either.
Stooping at the grate, gathering auld ash

always leaving a wee bed of ash
for the next fire's blazing dreams.
Heeking a' that heavy coal from the bunker.

The big black jewels in the steel bucket.
Toast from the naked flame was a treat,
or burning pink and white marshmallows

till they caved in and surrendered.
But that was rare.
This is what I most remember:

the time when Snowie, our school hamster,
comes home for a weekend holiday with me.
A cage is a cage no matter where the house is,

thinks Snowie, probably; so come nighttime
she escapes her prison, come nighttime
she fancies a night in a slumberdown,

climbs up the chimney breast
into the ma and da's bed.
You should have heard them scream

when they woke to see Snowie,
now the colour of soot, no snaw,
running the course of the duvet.

They were big screams, like this:
AAAAAAAAAAAAAAAAAAAAAAAAAAAAAA
AAAAAAAAAAAAAAAAAAHHHHHHHHHHHH

I spent the rest of the weekend
tight-lipped and desperate,
sponging that hamster with all my might

my wee yellow sponge going like a wiper,
hearing children chant in my ears,
She's made our Snowie into a darkie.

I tried and tried to make Snowie white.
It wis an impossible task.
Have you ever tried to shammy a hammy?

Monday morning wis an absolute disgrace.
I'll never forget the shame of it.
The wee GREY hamster looking po-faced.

Compound Fracture

That day
after the bone came through my skin –
my mother's voice split open

right into my ear, saying my name,
and then saying her own, on a phone not there;
not herself, using a strange tone.

It is her. I screamed for her, desperate.
She was in the next room repeating our names
until the nurse

burst into the white casualty
her eyes bulging with cruelty; a terse –
Now Now Now, her voice hailstones

pelting – *You won't be seeing your mother*
unless you button
that thick lip, and worse, worse.

So walls came in.
I tried to fasten
every button along my bottom lip, down to my

poisoned apple. I realized what
the nurse had said only by looking
at her body and her lips:

the starched white
of her uniform; her tight fitting
mouth; her polished black shoes. Whips.

That sardonic tongue; that regiment cap.
My mother was still in another world, taking sips
of sweet tea for shock; I ached for her soft lips.

Hottentot Venus

They made a plaster cast of my corpse
took wax moulds of my genitals and anus,
my famous anomalous buttocks
till the last sigh in me left my body.

I made a noise I never heard before
when the man with the glinting knife
whispered 'posterity' and dissected my brain.
Not so long ago people paid handsomely

to see my rump, my apron, my non-European genitals.
Two shillings. I paced my cage, backwards,
an orang-utan, forwards, a beast on a chain.
Men said the size of my lips were unnatural.

You can see the moulds of my genitals
at the Musée de l'Homme – Paris;
the rest of me is here now, Natural History Museum,
my brains, my woolly hair, my skeleton.

Some things I will never forget
no matter how I am divided up:
the look on a white lady's face
when she poked her parasol into my privates.

Her gloved hands. Her small stone eyes.
Her English squeal of surprise at my size.
My sigh is black. My heart is black.
My walk is black. My hide, my flanks. My secret.

My brain is the size of a black woman's brain.
When the gentleman prodded me with his cane

he wanted to discover black tears falling
from my dark eyes. I tell no lies.

Then he called my tears crocodile tears.
What did he call my lips? Rubber? Blubber?
My country is a dream now. Or maybe it did not exist.
When they called me in, three men in suits,

they asked me in my own bush tongue
if I wanted to be exhibited in this fashion.
I said the English words I'd heard them say often.
Money. Freedom. My Boer keeper smiled.

He could still walk me, dance me
hold his stick to me. He promised me riches.
Bring in the literati, the artists, the famous.
Let them view the buttocks of the Hottentot Venus.

My heart inside my cage pounded like a single drum.
For eleven hours a day people came to see Saartjie Baartman.
I heard their laughter like money shaking in a tin.
On the wall I was framed: ugly, deformed, a cartoon.

I was wearing a thin skin-coloured dress.
Hottentot Venus. Don't miss the Hottentot.
Now, what name have I got?
Sarah Bateman. Like an English woman. A great actress.

Christian Sanderson

Oor plan wis tae mak the clockmaker fu, fu
so's he wouldnie recognize me,
Bell or young Grace Thompson.
I sends oot fir mair malt whisky
bought wey the master clockmaker's shilling.
I'm shoor he wis expecting favours:
Grace wis the bait I used to lure him
doon the wynd they cry Hattie's close,
into the tenement. She's blonde and skinny
wey even, guid sized breasts.
I'm tae auld for a' that muck
an Bell wid rather pick a pocket or twa

fir a fine silk handkerchief
a guid gold watch or half a crown
than let a man like the clockmaker tak her.
And wha kin blame her. A' that depravity.
Men's filth and dirt and beerie breath.
Rank wey tobacco and stale herring.
Folk used to come by Christian Sanderson
to keep clean. I did a guid honest wash.
I didnae mak much. Onybody can find a tub. Soap.
My daughter wis starving the day o' the clockmaker.
Ten years auld and licking her lips like a cat.

There wis a frowsy blight on the window panes.
The gas lamps were blawing light on the auld toon.
The clockmaker was well abune the mu
when I knocked him doon and rifled his trousers.
Bell sat on him, pinned his arms. Tickled his chin.
I ran my big laundry hands thru his pants.
But his big cape, tho' fu o pockets,

had nae notes, jist a mouldy old sandwich.
Bell and I had to share 16 shilling.
Bell wis that disappointed she wis blazing:
'Bloody stupit rich auld fool coming oot
wey no money. Hardly a blastit fortune.'

Man robbery. Robbery from the person.
Seven years. Transportation. Australia.
It's a long word. Au stra li a.
When I heard my sentence in Edinburgh
I just aboot passed oot.

They said I wis a thief by habit.
What kin o habit's hungry, bony?
I got hot around the back o my heid. Dizzy.
I wondered whether I'd survive thon
terrible boats they pit you on
or if I'd arrive in the upside doon
lan' deid and dun. 'The mulatto's a thief by repute.'
That word I hate — mulatto. The Mulatto this,
the mulatto that. I felt like saying,
'My name is Christian Sanderson.'
I kept ma lips pursed thegither.
I looked doon at ma broon hands, crossed ma fingers.
Whit's going tae happen tae my daughter?

If that drunken clockmaker
had no remembered
I'd no be in this position;
or if I had decent employment at onything.
I wid hae worked if I could ha found it.
I'm no shirker. I wid hae sweated in ony workshop.

Men that make clocks remember things.
Women that suffer sullen poverty want tae forget things.
At the end of the lang day nothing's worth sixteen shillings.

Crown and Country

When you come to our country
you will realize we are big on dentistry:
at the border your mouth will be opened, flossed
and an elegant silver filling stamped into D 10.
Then you will catch the hygienic autobus, TOOTH
FAIRY EXPRESS, smiling the improved smile of our people

who all know dentures are more crucial
than culture. We do not talk much, we say
cheese; pints of creamy gleaming teeth,
pouring out our white grins, our gold caps; smirks.
Just across the border, people have hellish holes,
gaping gaps, rotten roots, abscesses.

We identify people by their bite.
The lower class have most unusual bites.
They are sick to the back teeth.
At 2 a.m. on a hot dusty night in our town
you will hear the fraught percussion
of the entire population grinding its teeth.

Our dentists are the richest in the world,
mining our gobs of gold. They love the old;
the ones who finally succumb to receding gums,
to teeth falling haplessly out like hailstones.
Be careful of the wind; it can make your mouth fly wide.
All along this natural canal, you will note,
our wild poppies pout; lush red lips.

Teeth

This is X who has all her own teeth.
Her mother is horrified by this.

Look into her mouth. She still has them.
Perfect pearls. Milk stones. Pure ivory.

Not a filling, no receding gums.
X was a woman with a lively

smile. Since she was a girl. No dark holes.
Her mother wore, still does, false teeth. Tusks,

badly fitted, left something unsaid
– a tiny gap between tooth and gum.

Her mum's teeth, in a glass tumbler, swam
at night: a shark's grin; a wolf's slow smirk.

What upsets her mother now, oddly,
is this: X had such beautiful lips.

This morning the men broke in – 8 a.m.
X was wearing her dressing gown, white

towelling. They came wearing her number
on their arms. *Did you know,* her mother says,

they taped my daughter's mouth to choke her
screams. They covered her mouth in white tape.

The small boy pulled at the sharp trousers.
He was soundless. The big men flung him

into that grey corner. His voice burst.
He will stand there, that height, forever, see

those minutes grab and snatch and repeat
themselves. The men in plain clothes have claws;

they attack his mother like dogs, gagging her,
binding her, changing her into someone

else. He will watch her hands smash and thrash.
His hands making a church, then a tall

steeple. He crosses his fingers. Squeezes them.
His hands wet themselves. He is five years old.

He knows his address. He knows his name.
He has ten fingers. He counts them again.

This is X who has all her own teeth.
Came to this country with her own teeth.

Soundbites will follow. Lies will roll
tomorrow. The man with the abscess

will say she had a weak heart. High blood.
Illegal. Only doing his job.

Fill it in. Write it down. Bridge the gap.
Give him a stamp of approval: silver

or gold or NHS, she resisted arrest;
there's your cause of death. On a plate.

She was wrong. Give her a number. Think
of a number. Take away the son.

Merle Collins

The Form

I remember the form of my guilt
the blackness of the dotted line
on the white paper. Name, okay.
Nationality? Pen poised to begin
Hand encircling paper, eyes wandering

Friend looks up from frowning at the form
of her search. Well, Name filled in
Nationality Trinidadian. Hers, a simple
assertion. I hold my breath, hoping
not to be reminded that I, complete with

Irish name, like hers, am not yet Grenadian
but still British. Her own pen poised
she struggles with another mammoth problem.
Race? She looks at my hand, over and around
at the pencilled African. Giggles, grins,

says with a kind of questioning awe, I put
Black. We shrug, look at each other, caught
in this dilemma of expressing some belonging.
Aspiring social-scientists, we look at the next
dotted line on the tutor's form. Social strata?

You put Lower class? We giggle. We grin.
Sitting on the balcony, encircled by the walls
of the region's university, two of the privileged
few, unsure of much, sure of search. Feeling
the birth pains of moulding a future belonging.

I remember the form of the past
foretelling the shape of things to come.

Nabel String

The part of me
that is there, not here
home, not wandering
not hey, how you doing?
but doodoo darling, you awright?

Not going up to this enclosed home
in the elevator, on stairs, in silent
unconcerned, instinctive hostility
with the neighbour I do not know
not turning the key for the umpteenth time
in the door of number 204 and suddenly
pausing, intent, attention on 203
I wonder who livin there? Not that
absence of you, of me, of warmth, of life,

but running outside with the piece of bread
Ay! Teacher Clearie! Shout the bus for me, nuh!
Ay! James! Wait! Take the kerosene pan!
I not taking no damn kerosene pan!
Eh! But he ignorant, eh!
Awright awright! Bring it! Ka dammit!

There, where neighbour is friend and enemy
to be cussed and caressed
so damn annoying you could scream sometimes
so blasted fast in you business
you could hate, most times
but when you're far away
hate is a memory of feeling
Loving and cussing and laughing and needing

is living. That blank stare from the unknown
next door neighbour kills something inside

And the sound that pulls
is of the heart beat, of the drum
beat. Is River Sallee, is a drummer
soaring, is Victoria, is Belmont,
those places that you, I, we left
Left to search, as always, for a better life
Left, sometimes, just because of a need to search
for the reason, the beginning, the end, the all.
So left, and will always be leaving
Left, too, to escape the lime
by the place they call the kwésé, by the L'anse
by the market. Left to find jobs, to chase education.

Go on child, take what I didn't get, you hear
I have no money to leave. All I have
is in you head. Left, too, because every year
more out of school, less work to get
because chemistry in fifth form this year
and standing on market hill straight
for the whole of next year
just didn't kind of make no sense.

Left, too, because love turned hate
is bitter, not sweet
Because the landless somehow becoming
more landless yet but still loving
some leader because of a memory
Left sometimes because things not so good
and something better is always somewhere else
Left because even if things going all right
the world big, and home is a feeling you're seeking

but in this new speaking, in the elevator, the lift
from over the sea there's the pull of the heart beat
of the drum voice. Ay! Bury the child nabel
string under the coconut tree, you know
by where I bury she father own!
So the nabel string there
and as the palm branch swaying

It pulling, it pulling, it pulling

The Beat Goes On

The beat goes on
and the planet's poor die
or slink off with a look of guilt and fear
guilty of sins un-named, non-existent.
The meek waiting to inherit the earth.
The taste of failure bitter in the mouth.
Who wants to be born to perch
huddled together over the river
in huts waiting to fall, begging to be seen

by big houses on the other side? All children
of that same distant God, some more equal

than others. And the big man shakes his head
and says, these people, man, they have no ambition.
Perhaps he knows that the eye of the needle will expand,
that the camel will enter to secure his heaven.
And the wretched scream, tired of waiting
to inherit the earth. Perhaps that scream will expand
like the eye of the imaginary needle, will reshape and create
some other kind of beauty. Perhaps then the wretched shall be
peacemakers, to inherit all kingdoms, all kingdoms present
all kingdoms to come.

A Friend

He's an artist, my friend
A poet, no less

He's the kind, he tells me
whose heart may shout in some
revolution's raging but hands won't
go up in vulgar display of emotions

no rushing cry of forward
no stinging revolutionary shout
though the thought may be there
the feeling, he says, even deeper

than many a shouted support.
May be happy with the dog, my friend,
not with its bite, so will nod at the lick
and wince at the snap, won't lick no

asses to summon the praise. He's a poet,
he tells me, an artist, no less

Be Free

My dream of ships, of people
of waiting decks and eager lines
moving towards distress, it seems

too soon awake, perhaps
but still, better the unfinished dream
than distressing news, better to destroy
the image fashioned by a mind eager
to drink the heady draught of shared creation
awed by the lilting tilt of the free bird's wing

the sibilant flow of beauty on the wing
but unable to release my particular bird
to wing its way

away

to sunlit creation. Grasping with greedy fingers
the beauty I love to watch, fascinated, released
and flowing. Loving freedom and beauty

in abstract, yet wanting to capture the essence
watching the caged bird, hoping to enjoy
the beauty of the bird on the wing. But the caged
bird wilts, losing that sibilance.
Through unreasoning fear I destroy the beauty
I want to hold. So now I release and watch you soar

try not to mind that your life is yours. I watch
you fall and hurt and mend your wing and dance
and falter and dip and soar and curtsy your own love
of life and love in answer to my prayer. Winging

away

into the startling, blinding sunlight
to make true my dream of ships which did not sail.
Still, no distress, I guess. Beauty unchained, on the wing.

Butterfly

Feeling sometimes like a butterfly
trapped
wings open, poised for flight
caught
by more than the matter seen
touched
by a need to know where history been
wanting
to find out where they make the fire
that melt the steel
that make the prison
to hold all those butterflies
that were made for flight

Fear

Afraid
must have been born afraid

turned around and refused to come out
till forced by the surgeon's knife
to look at the light, to scream
for fear of those shifting shadowed shapes

afraid
must have been born afraid

still at the corner of a clamouring world
assuming a calm in the teeth of the storm
afraid of the love that binds and demands
fearing those bonds that assume and control

afraid
must have been born afraid

timidity fed by blessings for the meek
chanting faith and hope while nursing
despair, reaching for warmth but afraid
of the strife that closeness could bring

afraid
must have been born afraid

Behind Shutters

I knew I had heard it somewhere before
He wrote that his father lived behind shutters
like 'if once you let yourself care
the crying might never stop'

and listening to the printed word
I looked back over the years
at a friend's face absorbing the shocking
idea that a person might not like to be liked

and I still believe I know
that whether you admit or not to caring
once you let yourself care
for the abstract or the live

the crying might really never stop
but then again, who knows?

The joy might never end

The Signs

I could tell from that time of trouble, long ago
that when some secret despair under there brewing
dogs have a way of knowing, weeks before

dogs look up, crying shame and howling horror
mourning in high hot sun with the blue sky turning red
going yellow, swimming in colour people never see before

the dogs knew

sometimes I wonder if is really that they hearing
spirit from long time screaming and caterwauling
or if is just dog-knowledge that have them howling

that dog passing on talk from under some chair
so is them have the whole story well early, because dog
howling story to dog and dog-drum message fulling up the air

whatever it is, the dogs knew

lying down, taking kick, and when talk hot, stepping out
to howl to their friends how they can't believe, how they
hoping talk of evolution not true, how not

all skin-teeth is good grin, how things gone sour, how big man
and woman can't swallow their pride, so the hour of
destruction is nigh, how all they could do in this trouble

is howl. Believe me, the dogs knew

and with dog howling so, the spirits that
turning in their grave get more bold, decide
to come out. And people say how their heart

beat to kill when they see a little something like a man
walking and moaning and crying in the night, bawling how some
human cut it down from some tree house that is home

I tell you, the dogs and the spirits did well know

and that was long before human hearing anything
to make them start bawling. So who know? Perhaps if people
had a habit of listening, some other something

might have come to pass. But then people say what is to is
must is. But look at that, eh! Look how in this tower of
babel, most of us, is only one language we know how to talk.

All I know is, looking back at it now, one thing that sure
is that before talk break, before thing turn ole mass
I tell you, the dogs and the spirits did know

A Memory

I remember touching your face, comrade
with anxious eyes.
I remember watching the quick shake
of your shoulders
the smooth flick of your fingers
stripping the weapon
I remember you looking up to say
Ready to roll, sister
Ready for any mad-ass mercenary that want to die
a sunshiny death this day.

I remember your hope, comrade
I remember your dreams
I remember your certainty of success, comrade
I don't want to remember your screams.

Interlude

As always, darkness follows the light
rainbow beauty, a spirit creation of fancy
and there I go willing beauty where none exists
watching molehills, willing mountains into shape

and now, shouldn't really cry for a dream unknown
for a wish not yet born, for brilliance imagined
by a mind eager to claim the power of creating miracles
Perhaps there was no real touch, just wander-lust

and now he can smile the famous victory style
as another one bites the dust. Curtain closed,
a chapter gone. Interlude over, story done
Command performance, applause, bow, curtain drawn.

The Cloud

The sun does funny things sometimes, dips
behind a non-existent cloud and the lights
we never knew were there go out

we feel the difference, yearn for the light
which we took for granted, yet hate this yearning
as dependence. We yearn, the sun doesn't even know it

but then we learn to do funny things sometimes, to turn
away when the sunlight goes and find some power to shine
so that the lights we never knew were there come up

The End

What's in your mind when mine is mixed
and angry and confused and wondering and needing
what hurts is this sensing that there's nothing there
that we're together at all because of my will

that really you are accepting of
whatever. Watching, not participating
shared with, not sharing, not
violently opposed, so not stopping

and they tell me that's not unusual
for the species. And so we go on
and one day perhaps I will say okay,
it's over. And you would have conceded

to my pride the victory which you won, long ago
without shout, without declaration, without show.

Long after the Beginning

Is it weariness that makes me not long for your returning?
Is it weariness that makes me cringe when you arrive?
Is it weariness that makes me watch the lips so closely
that I do not hear the laughter?
Is it weariness that makes me listen to the sound so closely
that I do not hear the words?
Is it weariness that makes me hug the corners
when the crowd comes rushing in?
Is it weariness that makes me walk more slowly now?
That makes me laugh less freely now?
That makes me move less eagerly now?
Is it weariness that keeps me staring
at the corners of your smile?
Perhaps. I think I'm just tired, really.

When It's All Over

When it's all over
while you're regretting its going
don't you wonder sometimes
at its staying so long?

Perhaps he had said well now
show me your motion
and you thought well, okay
tra-la-la-la-la
or in these days when things
don't really follow the yesterday way
perhaps even the other way round
in the ring
but still some kind of a
tra-la-la-la-la

all those days of striving
just to keep him wanting
didn't you wonder sometimes
about you perhaps wanting
more than just his judging
perhaps even doing some judging
yourself? Or were you just lulled
by the consistent chanting
of the tra-la-la-la-la?

And then when you stopped hurting
at his going, and had taken to thinking
again, was it then frightening
this no longer caring
this marvel of remembering
the tra-la-la-la-la?

And isn't it baffling and releasing
this daily discovering
that so much of loving
is more a consequence
of fear of loneliness
than sudden discovery of love?

Doesn't it leave you afraid
to keep watching the motion
to keep singing the singing
to keep chanting the chanting
of the tra-la-la-la-la?

Or do you just do some thinking
some simmering, some shrugging
some canny surviving
and end up deciding
well, cho, tra-la-la-la-la?

Disappointment

Perhaps you don't know it
but I met you
several yesterdays ago
like the god I was taught to revere, you
are here in many different shapes and sizes

Only yesterday, I saluted your uniqueness
and perhaps you wouldn't understand this
but the reason I'm silent now
is because I said it all
when I met you, yesterday

How Times Have Changed

I remember how
in days long ago,
I would squeeze my eyes tight shut
and pray
tremblingly
Lord, make this relationship work out
even though he's awful sometimes
you know that truly he's beautiful
inside, Lord. Bring out the best in him
Make him be really beautiful
Lord, make this relationship work out
and sometimes, I even added, threateningly
Or I shall die, and waited for results.

How times have changed!

Now, meeting you
whom I quite fancy
I say simply
to the watching me
seems to me it would be quite nice
if something works. If he's beautiful
inside, let him pause. If he's as awful
as I suspect, I'll survive without the hassle
being alone can be quite beautiful, sometimes
loneliness when in company is a pain I've learnt
to fear. How times have changed! From that, to this
From then, to now. It's funny
and beautifully peaceful

the way times have changed.

Images

Remembering
images met from birth
images that marked out margins
before I knew of words, of meanings

faces ever present, faces mostly absent
forbidden shouts, forbidden search
images created in other people's mind-
lessness. Images wrapped in skin-tight

words like woman, weak as straw, coward
as fly, devious as Delilah. Hammer-
blows on the distant, ever present self
like, dat boy fou-fou, eh! he really

stupid. Just like a girl. And you know,
I laughed. And laughed again at, dat
person in front of me driving like a real
bèbè. I sure is a blasted woman

but woy! you don't see that girl how she
handle that car so beautiful! she good, boy!
Just like a man! Walk, then, within the patterns

I shape, after my image, within my likeness.
Images battering the receptive, ever-forming mind
remembering watching women, watching houses

watching his house, registered in his name,
of course. Your labour, for love and gratitude
for his presence, his labour, for wealth
and you, a peaceful person, would be quietly

violated, would not make the demands that bring
revolutions. You, a peaceful person, would keep
your weakness and cherish your chains. Remembering
watching women, labour without value, working

all day, working no place, working women, quietly
asking at end of week for another twenty dollars
please, to buy shoes for our Jim, working women
biting lips as he sucks his teeth, biting back

words forming blood at the corners of her cheeks
remembering our anger, our questions, why don't you
fight back? Hush, child, she used to say, sometimes

you have to play dead to see what funeral you will get
so used to the game that even after the funeral over
the parson gone home, we still thinking we only playing

dead. Looking wise, talking wise, acting stupid
mind touching tender distances, going through the movements
according to the script. Still not knowing that whatever

the struggle, until we make it different, the boss will
always win, will always register in his name the blood,
the sweat, the tears of workers, till workers claim

our worth. Reshaping meaning, values, caring
working towards the vision of a sharing beauty.
Reality that we will create if only, only if

we insist on equal worth.

Some Days, Mother

Some days, mother
when my thoughts are a tangle I cannot untie
when meanings are lost and I cannot say why
when the daily drudging is exhausting not fulfilling
when a hollow inside says I'm existing not living
Those days, mother
when life is a circle that keeps me spinning not moving

Who else in the world could I tell of the pain?
Who else in the world would understand the hurt?
Who else in the world would I simply know is sharing?
Who else in the world could so love me in weakness?
Who else, mother? who else?

Some days, mother
when the coming of morning is an intrusion I fear
when the falling of night fuels thoughts of despair
when prayer for some deeper believing
is a passion I cannot express
when the tolling of time seems so slow
and so pointless

Who else in the world could I tell of the hurt?
Who else in the world wouldn't think me insane?
Who else in the world could love me
just for the sake of loving?
Who else, mother? Who else?

Some days, mother
when I can find no meaning
even in your existence
when we quarrel and argue

and I really wish I never knew you
when I listen and look at you
and hope I'm not seeing my future
when some other searching
has fuelled rejection

Who else in the world
would just love me again without question?
Who else holds this feeling
that nothing I do can erase?
Who else is simply always there for my story?
Who else, mother? Who else?

Some days, mother,
when I go searching for this kind of loving you're giving
when I go giving this kind of loving you're teaching
It's like trying to hold
the rainbow that drinks in the river
It's like trying to hug
the moonlight that sits on the doorstep
It's like spinning around in circles
and challenging the sky to come falling

So mother, tell me
Who else knows the secret of this deeper loving?
Who else shares the miracle of such tender caring?
Who else is there that knows
of this unstinting supporting?
Who else, mother?
Who else?

The Chant

My grandmother's chant walks with me
Not because I will it but because it is

Iceland
and the Faroe Islands belong to Denmark

Somehow
with William the Conqueror and his children
these places and faces were hers
and mine to inherit

Iceland
and the Faroe Islands belong to Denmark

She would stride through the house
muttering
pausing to listen to some word
the radio announcer didn't say

She would turn and laugh, laugh
muttering not about the places she had walked
but about all those places that held her thoughts captive

She left me, in her unwritten will
so much that she had learnt

Iceland
and the Faroe Islands belong to Denmark

Visit to the Faroe Islands

Even now, here with me in the Faroe Islands
my grandmother walks, chanting
When the fog clears, she says
you will see the harbour, and she laughs
laughs as the boats cross and criss-cross
across the water. I hear her shouting, too
as the Viking inheritors taunt each other across
the misty grey-white water. When the fog clears,
she laughs, you will see the water.

What haunts is not the memory of sea
not trees that won't grow on these islands' rocks
not the birds or leaves or mountains
what haunts is a heartbeat that goes deeper
than pulsing thought.

Searching, she laughs,
isn't always for a root that can be pulled and
touched. Island is island, you think, eh
Sea is sea, you say. Child, sometimes sea is
for tourist, you know. Meself, is the mountain
I know and the nutmeg under the cocoa.
When the fog clears, she shouts, through
the whiteness, you will see the slate-grey water

A ship's shape shooting from the fog
startles me to dreams of stars and wishes
Foam leaps a white relief to slate-grey
and today, nostalgic, licks the lips of yesterday
A grass-topped house hushed and huddling
haunted by envy of a greener past

Water falls down the mountainside in these islands
like a promise. And everywhere birds walk on water
Miracle is revealed as what you see but cannot hold

And when the fog clears, my grandmother
laughs again, striding, muttering
Child, you going see the harbour, you know
and she turns, my grandmother
and walks again, chanting.
This kind of searching, you know, child
is never ever for something that
you could hold and touch
Some days are misty, foggy days
she whispers, from her spirit world
but keep walking, child, even here in the Faroes
When the fog clear, huh, you going see the light again

Seduction

When first I came wandering into this cold confinement
my friend talked about things I couldn't hear then
but listen to now when voices are louder
with distance brought closer

my sister, she said, you've come for a year
maybe two, but you'll stay, longer
Life's moving on, patterns are shifting
Times are just changing and my sister, she said

the longer you linger in this seductive dying
the more silent, you'll see, you'll become
Twenty years, she said, in this cold confinement
and every winter I'm packing to leave

Twenty years, she said, putting by a little
for the days that are coming, not living
these days that are going, have gone
twenty winters, she said, deciding to leave

and stop dreaming, start living, start hoping
again that times will be changing. Twenty
winters, she said, of wanting to cross
the Atlantic again, to that place of some kind

of homecoming again, but that's changing.
This place, she said, is the home of my children
so you see, the picture is shifting again
but still, you know, twenty winters of crying

to leave. But then, summer comes in
gloomy, but brighter. Life holding some promise
again. And I linger, longer, in this seductive
dying, this sad and sweet subsisting

and the more silent, it appears, I become.
Going home becomes harder, she told me
cold winter is homely. The fire replaces
the sun. And yet there's a longing

for those places that gave me a longing
for leaving. But what keeps me wandering
still? she wonders. New roots, new shoots
and home moving further away. My voice becomes

weaker, she told me, the hope of returning
grows fainter, till later, when older
when things will be better
but the white clouds are distant, and cold

black pride is a promise I keep
and the longer I linger, she said
in this seductive dying, the more silent,
my friend, I feel, I become. But perhaps,

she said, perhaps there is a foundation
that people like me have been building
perhaps I haven't just wilted
while others have shouted

perhaps I haven't just wasted
and waited. Perhaps, she said, my quiet,
determined surviving give shouting voices
their strength. Perhaps, she told me,

if I'm not too fanciful, your shouting, my friend
is only my silence intoned. But sister, I remember,
she pleaded, try not to linger too long
in this seductive dying, this sad and sweet subsisting

or the more silent, you'll see, you'll become.

It Crow Fire

Every so often on a moonlight night
when something he could only explain
in a story made him smile, walk high
want to talk in a really intimate kind of style
my uncle would appear on the top step
with a shout of sa sa mi oh!
and wait for a sa i yo?
or with a Tim! Tim!
and wait for a Bashe or a Bois seche!

and so, the wooden-silence would be broken
he would tell a story not so much from the beginning
as at the beginning. He would throw us a riddle like
Me father have a cock when it crow it crow fire!
And wait for, I know! I know! A gun
As it was, in the beginning we knew
but didn't know that we knew
for perhaps the father's cock crowing fire
was really the gunpowder's curse, remembered

but just knowing that my uncle could
tell the beginning when the moon made nonsense
of reality, people would wait for the light
and walk in its circle
with a Tim Tim! Bois seche!
And the stories would move to
You hear the latest?
Those on the hill selling up, you know
Going back to England.

Back? Is there they come from?
Well, kind of. The great, great, great
grandfather, you know. But I hear is not really
England, nuh. Is Ireland, yes. And in our innocence
we would say England, Ireland, same thing.
So if he going, what happen to the estate?
Selling up? Who buying? Is another story entirely
But tell me, you self, where your grand people from?
No place to go back to? Let's leave that story

Tongue and teeth don't laugh at good thing
Fire me one! Fire me another drink there!
And then, they would remember us and say
Oh children, you listening? Tim! Tim!
and even then, we knew the word
but didn't know that we knew
not until later, when uncle, his voice gone
quiet, his audience gone listening elsewhere, the moon
no longer lighting a jagged track through his eyes

lowered his gaze, put his hands in his pockets
turned his seeing from inside outside
and walked away in search of places
where they say real storybook stories are made
And once, years later, I went to see uncle
in a London flat, no step of its own
no space for beginnings, not even for happy rememberings
and when, reaching back, I called, sa sa mi oh!
my uncle lifted his head, listened, looked

at the darkening corner, seemed to see nothing
must have heard nothing, said nothing
but in this darkness I wanted to hear again
the word that my uncle had known so well

I wanted to see the track of the light
in his eyes again
wanted to hear the tone of a story remembered
in his voice again
Tim! Tim!

but the beginning was gone
my uncle gone silent
and after a while he buttoned the jacket
of his London Underground uniform
picked up his cap, walked towards the darkened
doorway, towards the steps, down to the misty
outdoors. Then he turned, found a word, framed a question
in this room in one of the places where real storybook
stories are made. So you want to hear story now?

he asked me. You young people, with your ideas,
all-you drunk. All-you joking. Look at that!
Is now they want to know story, yes.

Where the Scattering Began

Here, on the streets of London
where, some say, the scattering began
we come to find our faces again
We come to measure the rhythm of our paces
against the call of the Ghanaian drum that talks
against the wail of the mbira from Zimbabwe
that yields music to the thumbs
We come with faces denying names
gone English, Irish, Scottish
We come with hands that speak
in ways the tongue has forgotten
We come with intonations
that reshape languages we have been given
We come with eyes that tell a story
the brain cannot recall
We come with the blue of the sea so close
that we lift our eyes with yearning
to the emptiness of the skies
Some of us come with the memory of
forest sounds that we have never known
We all come speaking so simply
of complicated things. Here
when we recognize each other
on the streets of London
hands and eyes and ears
begin to shape answers
to questions tongue can find
no words for asking.

Shipmates – A Train Journey

I watched him as he entered
watched how he sat there
hands deep in pockets
face clenched in total black defiance
eyes moving now from nothing
to rove in angry unconcern
I watched how his lips relaxed
just barely
when his eyes passed my face
returned
relaxed
wondered if to recognize, perhaps
with cautious smile
moved again
with the easy coldness
born of lifelong practice
born of practical experience

but face not quite so clenched now
for silently he had recognized
another passenger whose averted eyes
could not possibly mean
offence at errant blackness

and as I recognized his pain
my mind wandered through his story
and loving him, I wondered
wondered so hard that when I looked up
the giant hand was pulling closed the doors

as the train left my station stop.
I wondered, went one stop further
travelled back with clenched faces black
and white. Wondered, found no sudden
answers, and wandered wondering home.

Multiculture Abroad

They want me to write a poem
a poem like the natives write
about sand and sea and sunshine
and exotica like that.

They want me to speak a poem
a poem like they say West Indians speak
about rice and peas and carnival and mango trees
and multicultural things like that.

They want me to perform a poem
a poem like they say the Blacks perform
with black english and tenor pans
and bongo drums and musical stuff like that

They want me to write a poem
a poem that would prove how multi culture is
and it makes me think about living here and
writing there and migratory stuff like that

The Lumb Bank Children

(After a week's workshop, with people of different cultures, at a house at Lumb Bank, Yorkshire, in the north of England, where, the story goes, children died working in the mills and fields in the nineteenth century.)

Today we walk here where once the miller walked
imprisoned in time
confined for a week to the beauty that is now.

In the valley the mist hardly ever lifts
the hands that hold that white blanket down
are children's hands, they say
and that wail that wanders nightly
on this December wind
is not a Christmas carol
but children howling an ancient hunger
around the mill-house
now a gaunt memory of a living graveyard.

Last night, while a child's mangled memory
moaned under the misty white
a ghost walked from ancient India's cotton-fields
moved tall and stately through this lonely
valley house, connecting.

Last night, while wailing carols
wandered in the whitening cold
a figure walked through time and space
from a water-mill somewhere
near a Caribbean cane-field, searching.

The restless ghost child sighed, sucked a thumb,
turned over in her valley bed, and slept.
Early this morning, the mist lifted slowly.
The waterfall shouted a story
louder than its voice.

Today we walk where once the miller walked
released in time
surrounded for a week by the beauty that is now.

Whose Story?

Walking now through the streets of this Britain
which you seek to save from the painful fate
of black invasion, I wonder
if mine had been the invading nation
would history just have shrugged
written the story upside down
left a different people clothed
in this distant arrogance?
Would black magic be perfect magic?
The black sheep the treasured child?
Would I be sitting now
making poetic music in another land
singing of a different theme
nursing perhaps another strife?
I wonder how it would have been?

Back to the Beginning

In Ghana, when we walked through the castle
at Cape Coast, the guide, not lifting his voice, said,

most of the people taken from here
are supposed to have gone to the Caribbean.

we looked at each other and didn't speak with words
the guard moved on, pointing, explaining

and we followed, in silence. If there really
has been a fall from some place called Eden, the curse

for humans must have been to use words that could never
really give true meaning; so we speak with silence about

the deeper things. Further along the coast, the guard said,
is Elmina. From there, people were taken mainly to Brazil.

And we walked towards the entrance of the castle at Cape
Coast. There was another, white, party, and their guide

suggested that we travel together. Our guide looked
from them to us and shook his head. This trip we would

make alone. And who knows what was the ancestral role
of this black guide who takes us through cave dungeons, which,

we are told, were packed with bodies, where bones were left
where uncovered graves were made, where whispers echo still

where we walk hunched inside, where we stand quiet inside
where we listen silent, walk through the darkness to the

gaping hole beyond. There, for us, there was daylight
with the sea's whispering thunder below. For them, they said,

more darkness in those days, for there the ship waited, with
men holding weapons, waiting to crow fire, to keep them
   moving

Up and down the deck, up and down the deck

Up and Down the Deck: A Children's Game

Here in this land, hemmed in by the sea
they always tell us, from experience,
that seawater have no branch
and so we play our sea-games on the land

haunted by the land, frightened by the sea
when we show our longing for the blue they shout
Children, seawater have no branch, you know

they watch us at our games, smile when on land we
commandeer a boat, find ourselves a captain,
when we shout, rock the boat with moving

Up and down the deck. Keep moving
children, stay on the land, you hear
seawater have no branch, you know

perhaps the past holds us more tightly than we know
no ship crossing the Atlantic now
The whip-lash is only our chosen captain's voice

Up and down the deck. Keep moving
Up and down the deck. Keep moving

laughing, we rush to galley, to quarterdeck, stop to dance,
stop to look, stop to listen for our canny captain's trickery,
stop to decide if survival lies on deck or overboard

Up and down the deck. Keep moving
Up and down the deck. Keep moving

Our eyes watch the hands but we listen for the voice
the hands may trick and speak our dying. Boom
overhead! The hands say go to galley but the yard

ducks swift and silent as death remembered.
Up and down the deck. Keep moving
and the frenzied song and stomp begins again

a story spawned, perhaps, from yesterday
written on pages that do not fade with time
a ship's journal brought to shore in a children's

game of life and death remembered. Boom overhead!
seawater, they always tell us, from experience
have no branch. So now, beached on these islands

listening to the sea's thundering whisper, watching
its changing waves, we play our frantic sea-games on the land.

The Political Embrace

When you hold each other close
for that eternal moment
when you touch with your faces
one cheek, the other

what do those lingering heartbeats
say? Do you think of love
for the hopeful ones you represent?
Or is that just the camera's suggestion?

As you touch, does hope scream some arrogant dream?
Do revolutions merge to touch the pulse
of something deeper? Or do you simply try,
to make people sleep to have, again, some vagrant dream?

To Trample Dreams

If you had moved beyond an early unbelief
if you had moved to trusting
if you had moved to stretching out your hand
to touch the warmth of that struggle
said to be for justice, for food, for education
if you had moved to believing that this struggle
of which so many spoke was your struggle

then your pain is my pain
your renewed unbelief is my distress

you, too, know with a wisdom newly born
of hurt that we can choose a golden platter
to hand away our dreams. Standing ant-like now
in a spinning, roaring chaos, become
so many Simon-Peters, so many Judases
we whisper again that we know not him
But, we say, ask that man there
this woman here, that is one of them

and even as you speak, I know that your pain
is my pain, your unbelief is my distress

and perhaps someone might give me
thirty or so shining pieces, please
After all, people must live
Someone, please, play the tunes
so I could dance a lively death-mask jig
I would be a very tender puppet
on your living string. I have heard tell
of people running, screaming, people
stepping movie steps over fifty foot walls
just because someone wanted them to trample dreams

They can kill our bodies, voices used to shout
in those days when the struggle was one struggle
they can never kill the spirit. And now
in this day of our distress, that they
has become a literary exercise
but perhaps, just perhaps, when
the rivers in these islands' mountains
come down and the bridges prove
too small to hold back the raging
those who used to believe in miracles
must believe again that there is

some other road. So much has been lost
but still there is so much to lose
In this hour of unbelief, the miracle
is that some time, somewhere, someone knew
that the darkest hour is just before the dawn.

Just Suddenly So

Always, after those hopeful beginnings
all of a sudden it not nice again
just suddenly so, with a funny kind of
reasonless reason, the experience turn sour
is no kind of adventure again.

Mouse-trap smiles clang suddenly shut.
The power-wand waves, sometimes, with
a gentleness suspect because employed and
withdrawn at will. Smiles come and go
Kicks, kisses, come, go, fly, live, die.

And bewildered, we silently vow to keep
screaming, low and loud, not to be caught
by gentleness idly tossed, idly withdrawn
To move, to grow, to live, to grow
to die and not to wilt, to shout

and insist on growing.

The Future

I look forward to the day
when, falling with a start
out of some dream of beauty,
I won't pull up the covers
and struggle to recall what's vanished
but welcome with a smile
the beauty that I find on waking.

Glimpses

lost the way, wandering star
spinning without motion
speeding, no direction
living this constant journey
a blur of decisive inactivity
dreading arrival in all this journeying
purposefully spinning pointlessly
and sudden glimpses of heaven
in this deafening chaos. Can recognize
that the end is the beginning. Can feel
the stillness of motion. Lost the way
just a constantly wandering star.

When Night Falls

When night falls
the women who create
and re-create stories
test the temper of the body

they groan with the pain
of moving
sigh
and declare

Well that is that
the body well tired
Thank the Lord for another
twenty-four hours

What gone well gone
Tomorrow is another day
When night falls
they bunch their skirts

and sink sighing to the steps
they fan their faces
and assert that the work
was good today

That last load of cane
that last bucket of stone
pull us through.
We make it.

They think of the child's teeth
of the school uniform
of the food for the week
they consider the budget

the day just ended
and declare
Well, that is that
they test the temper of the body

and decide
well time to put sleep to bed
Tomorrow is another day
When night falls

they stretch the body
and laugh at its hurting
these women who smile
they take time for a little remembering

Child, they say, things good today, yes
Let me tell you bout long time days
You think it was easy?
Let me tell you the story

And then, laughter massages
the body relaxes
Tongue, teeth and throat
enjoy re-creating

Let me just take
a little rest, they say
these women who weave
the stories

Let me rest first, you hear,
child, before going to sleep
Let me rest
Tomorrow is another day

The owl hoots, they cross themselves
move eyes to the door. It close?
It close? Make sure it close, you know
You hear the owl? Somebody going

I wonder who that? Close the door
Close the door
It ain't getting
no soul here tonight

And then they laugh at their fearing
They stretch, they yawn
Well, that is that, yes
Is only the day that dying

But we see another one through, yes
Thank the Lord. Let sleep go to bed
We'll see what tomorrow will bring
We'll see what tomorrow will bring.

A Dream

I remember the urgency
of the poem that I dreamt
I remember the pain
I remember the power
I remember the strain
I remember the hope
I remember the doubt
I remember the sadness
I remember the force

I remember the poem, you see
is just the words I forget.

Born Free

Born free
to be caught
and fashioned
and shaped
and freed to wander
in a caged dream
of tears

You Carry My Life

You carry my life
in the questions in your eyes
in the silence of your fears
in the anguish of your tears
when you let anyone stop you walking
my step falters
when you let them stop you talking
my voice becomes weaker
when you let them stop you looking
my eyes grow dimmer
when you let them stop you reasoning
my thoughts become confused
if you think anyone might stop you
wanting to re-create
look for the rest of us
you carry our lives
in the questions in your eyes
just like we carry yours

Grace Nichols

from I IS A LONG-MEMORIED WOMAN

NEW WORLD

Like the yesterday of creation morning
she had imagined this new world to be —
bereft of fecundity

No she wasn't prepared
for the sea that lashed
fire that seared
solid earth that delivered
her up
birds that flew
not wanting to see the utter
rawness of life everywhere

and the men who seed the children
she wasn't prepared for that look
in their eye

that loss of deep man pride

*

Now she stoops
in green canefields
piecing the life she would lead

*

And yet . . .
And yet . . .

the cutlass in her hand
could not cut through
the days that fell
like bramble

and the destruction that
threatened to choke
within

as she leaned closer to
the earth
seeking some truth
unarmed against the noon

*

We must hold fast to dreams
We must be patient
from the crouching of those huts
from the sprouting of these fields
We can emerge

all revolutions are rooted in dreams

*

We the women who toil
unadorn
heads tie with cheap
cotton

We the women who cut
clear fetch dig sing

We the women making
something from this
ache-and-pain-a-me
back-o-hardness

Yet we the women
who praises go unsung
who voices go unheard
who deaths they sweep
aside
as easy as dead leaves

　　　　*

Ibo/Yoruba
Ashanti/Fanti
Mane

each time they came
she went out to see
them
the new arrivals
faces full of old
incisions
calves grooved from
shackles
ankles swollen
from the pain

Each time they came
she made
as if to touch them
the new arrivals
her own lips
moving in a dreaming
kind of prayer . . .

TAINT

But I was stolen by men
the colour of my own skin
borne away by men whose heels
had become hoofs
whose hands had turned talons
bearing me down
   to the trail
of darkness

But I was traded by men
the colour of my own skin
traded like a fowl   like a goat
like a sack of kernels I was
traded
   for beads   for pans
for trinkets?

No it isn't easy to forget
what we refuse to remember

Daily I rinse the taint
of treachery from my mouth

WATERPOT

The daily going out
and coming in
always being hurried
along
like like . . . cattle

In the evenings
returning from the fields
she tried hard to walk
like a woman

she tried very hard
pulling herself erect
with every three or four
steps
pulling herself together
holding herself like
royal cane

And the overseer
hurrying them along
in the quickening darkness

And the overseer sneering
them along in the quickening
darkness
sneered at the pathetic
the pathetic display
of dignity

O but look
there's a waterpot growing
from her head

IN MY NAME

Heavy with child

belly
an arc
of black moon

I squat over
dry plantain leaves

and command the earth
to receive you

in my name
in my blood

to receive you
my curled bean

my tainted

perfect child

        my bastard fruit
        my seedling
        my sea grape
        my strange mulatto
        my little bloodling

        Let the snake slipping in deep grass
        be dumb before you

        Let the centipede writhe and shrivel
        in its tracks

        Let the evil one strangle on his own tongue
        even as he sets his eyes upon you

        For with my blood
        I've cleansed you
        and with my tears
        I've pooled the river Niger

        now my sweet one it is for you to swim

SUGAR CANE

1

There is something
about sugar cane

he isn't what
he seem —

indifferent hard
and sheathed in blades

his waving arms
is a sign for help

his skin thick
only to protect
the juice inside
himself

2

His colour
is the aura
of jaundice
when he ripe

he shiver
like ague
when it rain

he suffer
from bellywork
burning fever
and delirium

just before
the hurricane
strike
smashing him to pieces

3

Growing up
is an art

he don't have
any control of

it is us
who groom and
weed him

who stick him
in the earth
in the first place

and when he
growing tall

with the help
of the sun
and rain

we feel the
need to strangle
the life

out of him

But either way he can't survive

4

Slowly
pain-
fully
sugar
cane
pushes
his
knotted
joints
upwards
from
the
earth
slowly
pain-
fully
he
comes
to learn
the
truth
about
himself
the
crimes
committed
in
his
name

5

He cast his shadow
to the earth

the wind is
his only mistress

I hear them
moving
in rustling tones

she shakes
his hard reserve

smoothing
stroking
caressing
all his length
shamelessly

I crouch
below them
quietly

LIKE A FLAME

Raising up
from my weeding
of ripening cane

my eyes
make four
with this man

there ain't
no reason
to laugh

but
I laughing
in confusion

his hands
soft his words
quick his lips
curling as in
prayer

I nod

I like this man

Tonight
I go to meet him
like a flame

NIGHT IS HER ROBE

Night is her robe
Moon is her element

Quivering and alert
she's stepping out behind
the fields of sugarcane

She's stepping out softly
she's stepping out carefully
she's bending/she's stalking
she's flitting/she's crawling

Quivering and alert
she's coming to the edge
of her island forest

Now with all the care
of a herbalist
she's gathering strange weeds
wild root
leaves with the property
both to harm and to heal

Quivering and alert
Quivering and alert
she's leaving the edge
of her island forest

LOVE ACT

She enter into his Great House
her see-far looking eyes
unassuming

He fix her with his glassy stare
and feel the thin fire in his blood
awakening

Soon she is the fuel
that keep them all going

He/his mistresswife/and his
children who take to her breasts
like leeches

He want to tower above her
want her to raise her ebony

haunches and when she does
he think she can be trusted
and drinks her in

and his mistresswife
spending her days in rings
of vacant smiling
is glad to be rid of the
loveact

But time pass/es

Her sorcery cut them
like a whip

She hide her triumph
and slowly stir the hate
of poison in

SKIN-TEETH

Not every skin-teeth
is a smile 'Massa'

if you see me smiling
when you pass

if you see me bending
when you ask

Know that I smile
know that I bend
only the better
to rise and strike
again

OMEN

I require an omen, a signal
I kyan not work this craft
on my own strength

alligator teeth
and feathers
old root and powder

I kyan not work this craft
this magic black
on my own strength

Dahomey lurking in my shadows
Yoruba lurking in my shadows
Ashanti lurking in my shadows

I am confused
I lust for guidance
a signal, a small omen
perhaps a bird picking
at my roof

WIND A CHANGE

Wind a change
blow soft but
steadfast

ripple the spears
of sugar cane
stir slow the leaves
of indigo

Dance
waltz
soothe
this old mud-wattle
hut
bring if you can
the smell of Dahomey
again

Wind a change
cool mountain water
open river flower

But pass easy
up the big house
way
let them sleep
they happy white sleep

Yes, Wind a change
keep yuh coming fire
secret

EPILOGUE

I have crossed an ocean
I have lost my tongue
from the root of the old one
a new one has sprung

The Assertion

Heavy as a whale
eyes beady with contempt
and a kind of fire of love
the fat black woman sits
on the golden stool
and refuses to move

the white robed chiefs
are resigned
in their postures of resignation

the fat black woman's fingers
are creased in gold
body ringed in folds
pulse beat at her throat

This is my birthright
says the fat black woman
giving a fat black chuckle
showing her fat black toes

The Fat Black Woman Goes Shopping

Shopping in London winter
is a real drag for the fat black woman
going from store to store
in search of accommodating clothes
and de weather so cold

Look at the frozen thin mannequins
fixing her with grin
and de pretty face salesgals
exchanging slimming glances
thinking she don't notice

Lord is aggravating

Nothing soft and bright and billowing
to flow like breezy sunlight
when she walking

The fat black woman curses in Swahili/Yoruba
and nation language under her breathing
all this journeying and journeying

The fat black woman could only conclude
that when it come to fashion
the choice is lean

       Nothing much beyond size 14

Fat Poem

Fat is
as fat is
as fat is

Fat does
as fat thinks

Fat feels
as fat please

Fat believes

        Fat is to butter
        as milk is to cream
        fat is to sugar
        as pud is to steam

Fat is a dream
in times of lean

           fat is a darling
           a dumpling
           a squeeze
           fat is cuddles
           up a baby's sleeve

           and fat speaks for itself

Tropical Death

The fat black woman want
a brilliant tropical death
not a cold sojourn
in some North Europe far/forlorn

The fat black woman want
some heat/hibiscus at her feet
blue sea dress
to wrap her neat

The fat black woman want
some bawl
no quiet jerk tear wiping
a polite hearse withdrawal

The fat black woman want
all her dead rights
first night
third night
nine night
all the sleepless droning
red-eyed wake nights

In the heart
of her mother's sweetbreast
In the shade
of the sun leaf's cool bless
In the bloom
of her people's bloodrest

the fat black woman want
a brilliant tropical death yes

Thoughts Drifting Through the Fat Black Woman's Head
While Having a Full Bubble Bath

Steatopygous sky
Steatopygous sea
Steatopygous waves
Steatopygous me

O how I long to place my foot
on the head of anthropology

to swig my breasts
in the face of history

to scrub my back
with the dogma of theology

to put my soap
in the slimming industry's
profitsome spoke

Steatopygous sky
Steatopygous sea
Steatopygous waves
Steatopygous me

The Fat Black Woman's Motto on Her Bedroom Door

IT'S BETTER TO DIE IN THE FLESH OF HOPE
THAN TO LIVE IN THE SLIMNESS OF DESPAIR

Like a Beacon

In London
every now and then
I get this craving
for my mother's food
I leave art galleries
in search of plantains
saltfish/sweet potatoes

I need this link

I need this touch
of home
swinging my bag
like a beacon
against the cold

Winter Thoughts

I've reduced the sun
to the neat oblong of fire
in my living room

I've reduced the little
fleshy tongues of the vagina
to the pimpled grate
and the reddening licking
flames

I've reduced the sea
to the throbbing fruit
in me

And outside
the old rose tree
is once again winterdying

While I lay here sprawled
thinking
how sex and death
are always at the heart
of living

LAZY THOUGHTS OF A LAZY WOMAN

DUST

Dust has a right to settle
Milk the right to curdle
Cheese the right to turn green
Scum and fungi are rich words.

GREASE

Grease steals in like a lover
over the body of my oven.
Grease kisses the knobs
of my stove.
Grease plays with the small
hands of my spoons.
Grease caresses the skin
of my table-cloth,
getting into my every crease.
Grease reassures me that life
is naturally sticky.

Grease is obviously having an affair with me.

WHO WAS IT?

Who was it I wonder
introduced the hairless habit?
I have an interest
though I will not shave the armpit

No Gillette
I will not defoliage my forests

Also, let the hairline of the bikini
Be fringed with indecency
Let 'unwanted body hair' straggle free

O Mary Cant
O Estee Laud
O Helena Frankinstein

WITH APOLOGIES TO HAMLET

To pee or not to pee
That is the question

Whether it's sensibler in the mind
To suffer for sake of verse
The discomforting slings
Of a full and pressing bladder
Or to break poetic thought for loo
As a course of matter
And by apee-sing end it.

THE BODY RECLINING

With a thought for Walt

I sing the body reclining
I sing the throwing back of self
I sing the cushioned head
The fallen arm
The lolling breast
I sing the body reclining
As an indolent continent

I sing the body reclining
I sing the easy breathing ribs
I sing the horizontal neck
I sing the slow-moving blood
Sluggish as a river
In its lower course

I sing the weighing thighs
The idle toes
The liming* knees
I sing the body reclining
As a wayward tree

I sing the restful nerve

Those who scrub and scrub
incessantly
corrupt the body

*West Indian expression for standing around idling away the time.

Those who dust and dust
incessantly
also corrupt the body

And are caught in the asylum
Of their own making
Therefore I sing the body reclining

Configurations

He gives her all the configurations
of Europe.

She gives him a cloud burst of parrots.

He gives her straight blond hairs
and a white frenzy.

She gives him black wool. The darkness
of her twin fruits.

He gives her uranium, platinum, aluminium
and Concorde.

She gives him her 'Bantu buttocks'.

He rants about the spice in her skin.

She croons his alabaster and scratches him.

He does a Columbus –
falling on the shores of her tangled nappy orchard.

She delivers up the whole Indies again
But this time her wide open legs close in slowly

Making a golden stool of the empire
of his head.

Because She Has Come

Because she has come
with geometrical designs
upon her breasts

Because she has borne five children
and her belly is criss-crossed
with little tongues of fire

Because she has braided her hair
in the cornrow, twisting it upwards
to show her high inner status

Because she has tucked
a bright wrap
about her Nubian brownness

Because she has stained her toes
with the juice of the henna
to attract any number of arrant males

Because she has the good sense
to wear a scarab
to protect her heart

Because she has a pearl
in the middle
of her lower delta

Give her honour
Give her honour, you fools,
Give her honour.

Beverley's Saga

For Beverley and Jamaican dub-poet Jean Binta Breeze

Me good friend Beverley
Come to England. She was three.
She born in Jamaica, but seh,
Dis ya she country.
She ancestor blood help fe build it,
Dat is history.
Dih black presence go back
Two, three century.

She seh she fadder
Was minding he own business
Back in Jam-country,
Wid he lickle piece-o-land
An he lickle donkey
When dey sen he fe enlist
In de British Army.
Yes, he hads was to fight
Fe dis ya country.
Dey even give he medal fe bravery.

So policeman na come
Wid no brutality.
Mister Repatriation, yuh know,
You will haffi kill she
Cause she na go no whey
Dis ya she country.
Summer is hearts
An she dread de wintry
But she have she lickle flat
An she have she lickle key.

She seh she like it fine
She a pop wid style
You can never put she back inna no woodpile
Or she bun it to de ground.

She seh she went to Uncle Sam
For a six-week vacation,
But after three week
She homesick fe England.
When de plane mek a touch-down
She feel so happy,
She feel she a come home,
Dis ya she country.
If dey think bout repatriation
Dem will haffi kill she.

De odder day
Wan ole English lady stop she,
Seh, 'Miss are you on holiday?'
Bev seh, 'Me not on holiday,
Me a live right hey.
Me na plan fe go no whey.'

De ole lady open she eye, surprisedly,
Bev seh, 'Is Black British dey call we.'
She seh, 'I don't mean to be unkind
But leh me tell you lickle history —
You see all dis big fat architectry?
In it is de blood of my ancestry.
Dih black presence go back
Two, three century.
Don't look at me so bemusedly.'

Bev seh, 'In any case, you been my country first,
So we come back inna kinda reverse.
Isn't life funny? Dis ya. Dis ya history.
O mek we tek a lickle walk,
It so nice an sunny.
Summer is hearts,
An a dread de wintry.
But a have me lickle flat
An a have me lickle key.
You want to come in
For a lickle cup-o-tea?'

For Forest

Forest could keep secrets
Forest could keep secrets

Forest tune in everyday
to watersound and birdsound
Forest letting her hair down
to the teeming creeping of her forest-ground

But Forest don't broadcast her business
no Forest cover her business down
from sky and fast-eye sun
and when night come
and darkness wrap her like a gown
Forest is a bad dream woman

Forest dreaming about mountain
and when earth was young
Forest dreaming of the caress of gold
Forest rootsing with mysterious eldorado

and when howler monkey
wake her up with howl
Forest just stretch and stir
to a new day of sound

but coming back to secrets
Forest could keep secrets
Forest could keep secrets
      And we must keep Forest

Iguana Memory

Saw an iguana once
when I was very small
in our backdam backyard
came rustling across my path

green like moving newleaf sunlight

big like big big lizard
with more legs than centipede
so it seemed to me
and it must have stopped a while
eyes meeting mine
iguana and child locked in a brief
split moment happening
before it went hurrying

       for the green of its life

Blackout

Blackout is endemic to the land.
People have grown sixth sense
and sonic ways, like bats,
emerging out of the shadows
into the light of their own flesh.

But the car headlamps coming towards us
make it seem we're in some third world movie,
throwing up potholes and houses exaggeratedly,
the fresh white painted and grey ramshackle
blending into snug relief.

And inside, the children are still hovering,
hopeful moths around – the flickerless Box,
immune to the cloying stench of toilets
that can't be flushed. The children,
all waiting on electric-spell to come
and trigger a movie, the one featuring America,
played out endlessly in their heads.

While back outside, coconut vendors decapitate
the night, husky heads cutlassed off
in the medieval glow of bottle lamps.

And everywhere there are flittings
and things coming into being,
in a night where footfall is an act of faith –
a group of young girls huddled
in a questionable doorway;
The sudden dim horizontal of an alleyway;
And the occasional generator-lit big house,

obscenely bright –
hurting the soft iris of darkness
in this worn-out movie, slow reeling

Under the endless cinema of the skies.

Abra-Cadabra

My mother had more magic
in her thumb
than the length and breadth
of any magician

Weaving incredible stories
around the dark-green senna brew
just to make us slake
the ritual Sunday purgative

Knowing when to place a cochineal poultice
on a fevered forehead
Knowing how to measure a belly's symmetry
kneading the narah pains away

Once my baby sister stuffed
a split-pea up her nostril
my mother got a crochet needle
and gently tried to pry it out

We stood around her
like inquisitive gauldings

Suddenly, in surgeon's tone she ordered,
'Pass the black pepper,'
and patted a little
under the dozing nose.

My baby sister sneezed.
The rest was history.

Wherever I Hang

I leave me people, me land, me home
For reasons, I not too sure
I forsake de sun
And de humming-bird splendour
Had big rats in de floorboard
So I pick up me new-world-self
And come, to this place call England
At first I feeling like I in dream –
De misty greyness
I touching de walls to see if they real
They solid to de seam
And de people pouring from de underground system
Like beans
And when I look up to de sky
I see Lord Nelson high – too high to lie

And is so I sending home photos of myself
Among de pigeons and de snow
And is so I warding off de cold
And is so, little by little
I begin to change my calypso ways
Never visiting nobody
Before giving them clear warning
And waiting me turn in queue
Now, after all this time
I get accustom to de English life
But I still miss back-home side
To tell you de truth
I don't know really where I belaang

Yes, divided to de ocean
Divided to de bone

Wherever I hang me knickers — that's my home.

Loveday and Ann

Two women with a basket of flowers by Frances Hodgkins, 1915, Tate Gallery

One has rolled away –
unwinding in the waves
or her private blue ocean,
knowing how right she is.
The beauty of her smugness –
Not lost on the other who sees
the pleasure of her crabbing-hand
but chooses to stay land-locked,
sulking on the sands of her own
small hurt. While flowers bear witness –
Even in the alcove of friendship
there are distances.

Acknowledgements

The poems in this selection are taken from the following books, to whose publishers acknowledgement is made: *The Adoption Papers* (Bloodaxe, 1991), *Two's Company* (Puffin, 1992), *Other Lovers* (Bloodaxe, 1993) and *Three Has Gone* (Puffin, 1994) for Jackie Kay; *Because the Dawn Breaks* (Karia Press, 1985) and *Rotten Pomerack* (Virago, 1992) for Merle Collins; *I is a Long-memoried Woman* (Karnac House, 1983), *The Fat Black Woman's Poems* (Virago, 1984) and *Lazy Thoughts of a Lazy Woman* (Virago, 1989) for Grace Nichols.